The Library of SPIDERS

The Wolf Spider

Alice B. McGinty

The Rosen Publishing Group's
PowerKids Press™
New York

To Zachary

Published in 2002 by The Rosen Publishing Group, Inc.
29 East 21st Street, New York, NY 10010

First Edition

Book Design: Emily Muschinske
Project Editor: Emily Raabe

Photo Credits: title page, p. 10 (top) © Michael Cardwell; p. 5 © Animals Animals; p. 6 (top) © Robert Noonan; p. 6 (lower) © Joe Mc Donald/Animals Animals; pp. 9, 10 (middle), pp. 11, 17 (bottom), p. 21 (bottom), p. 22 © James P. Rowan; p. 10 (bottom) © Paul Berquist/Animals Animals; p. 13 (right) © A. B. Sheldon; p. 13 (left) © John Anderson/Animals Animals; p. 14 © Paul Freed/Animals Animals; p. 15 © Animals Animals; p. 17 (top) © Charles Palek/ Animals Animals; p. 18 (left) © Roger Regeot/David Liebman; p. 18 (right) © Bill Beatty/Animals Animals; p. 21 (top) © Michael and Patricia Fogden/CORBIS.

McGinty, Alice B.
    The wolf spider / Alice B. McGinty.— 1st ed.
        p. cm. — (The library of spiders)
    ISBN 0-8239-5567-2 (lib. bdg.)
    1. Wolf spiders—Juvenile literature. [1. Wolf spiders. 2. Spiders.]
I. Title
    QL458.42.L9 M35 2002
595 4'4—dc21

Manufactured in the United States of America

Contents

The Wolf Spider

There are close to 2,000 **species** of wolf spiders. Some species of wolf spiders live in far off places, such as the **Arctic** or in the **tropics**. Other species live as close as your own backyard. They make their homes around rocks, in grasses, and in piles of leaves. Wolf spiders also live in deserts, forests, prairies, and on sandy beaches.

Wolf spiders are usually dark brown or gray, and very hairy. The smallest species of wolf spiders are about one fourth of an inch (.64 cm) long. The largest are almost two inches (.5 cm) long, including their legs.

(Right) Wolf spiders are very furry, with big eyes.

Did You Know?

Wolf spiders are found in every single part of the world except on the continent of Antarctica. Wolf spiders can even live in extremely cold places like the Arctic, and high up on mountains.

joint

(Below) Wolf spiders have many different markings, but most are a brownish color. Even with its babies on its back this wolf spider matches the bark on which it is climbing.

(Above) This picture shows where the legs attach to the spider's body.

A Spider Like a Wolf

Scientists divide plants and animals into groups so they can study them. The members of each group are alike in certain ways. All spiders belong to a large group of animals called **anthropods**. Anthropods have a hard covering on their bodies called an **exoskeleton**. They also have **joints** that help their legs bend.

Wolf spiders also belong to a smaller group, or family, of spiders called Lycosidae. The word Lycosidae comes from the Greek word for wolf. Wolf spiders are like wolves in several ways. Like wolves, most wolf spiders are hunters, chasing their prey instead of catching it in a web. Wolf spiders also have hairy bodies like wolves. Wolf spiders and wolves both use their keen eyesight to spot prey. Finally, wolf spiders have strong jaws and sharp fangs, like wolves. Wolf spiders use their strong teeth to chew their prey.

The Wolf Spider's Body

The wolf spider has two main body parts, the **cephalothorax** and the **abdomen**.

The cephalothorax is the front half of the spider's body. The spider's brain and stomach are inside. Spiders' legs are attached to the cephalothorax.

The spider's abdomen is behind the cephalothorax. It contains the spider's heart, lungs, **silk glands**, and **spinnerettes**. In most spiders, the abdomen is bigger than the cephalothorax. In wolf spiders, the two parts are about the same size.

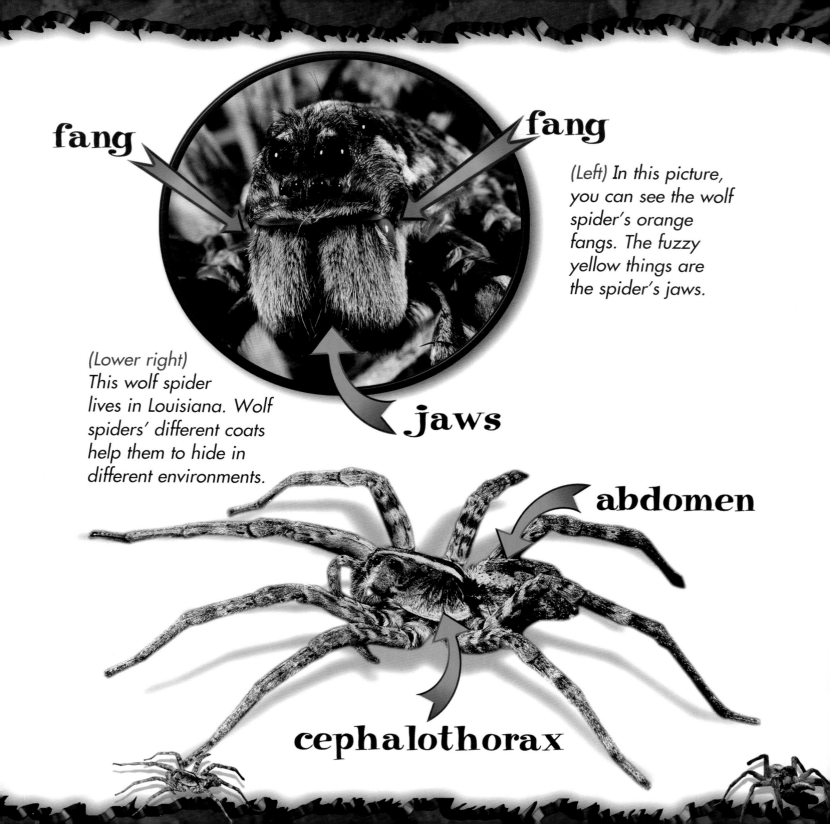

fang

fang

(Left) In this picture, you can see the wolf spider's orange fangs. The fuzzy yellow things are the spider's jaws.

(Lower right) This wolf spider lives in Louisiana. Wolf spiders' different coats help them to hide in different environments.

jaws

abdomen

cephalothorax

Many wolf spiders hunt at night. They have reflectors in their eyes to help them see in the dark. These reflectors make the spider's eyes seem to glow in the dark.

The Wolf Spider's Senses

Because most wolf spiders are hunters, their vision is better than most spiders. The wolf spider has eight eyes. A row of four small eyes faces forward. Above them are four bigger eyes. Two of them face up and two face sideways. This helps the wolf spider see in many directions.

The wolf spider's body is covered with hairs. When something, like an insect or an animal, moves the air or ground, the spider's hairs **vibrate**. In this way, the spider senses touch and vibration.

(Right) This picture shows the wolf spider's many eyes.

11

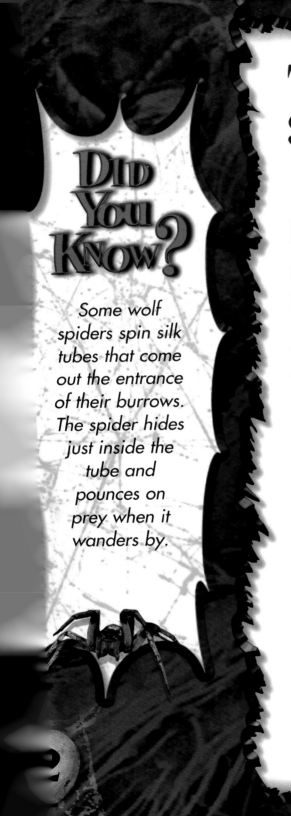

Did You Know?

Some wolf spiders spin silk tubes that come out the entrance of their burrows. The spider hides just inside the tube and pounces on prey when it wanders by.

The Wolf Spider's Home

Wolf spiders have many kinds of homes. Some species dig burrows underground. As the spider digs its burrow, it may wrap clumps of dirt or sand in silk. The silk makes it easier for the spider to carry the dirt out of its burrow. The spider may also use silk to line the sides of its burrow.

Other kinds of wolf spiders live under stones, in the bark of trees, or buried underneath snow. Some wolf spiders do not have homes at all, but wander from place to place. Each species has learned the best way to survive in its surroundings.

(Above) This is a wolf spider's burrow.

(Left) This tropical wolf spider spins a sheet-like web for its home.

Hunting Prey

Most wolf spiders are hunters. They wander in search of small insects to eat. Some wolf spiders hunt during the day. Others hunt at night.

The wolf spider creeps up close to its prey. Then the spider pounces on the insect, and bites it with its fangs. Wolf spiders pounce very quickly and powerfully. The wolf spider crushes the insect with its teeth until the insides are soft. Then the spider sucks out the juices of its victim, leaving behind only the crushed shell.

(Left) This wolf spider is eating a tadpole.

(Right) This wolf spider is crushing its prey in its powerful jaws.

15

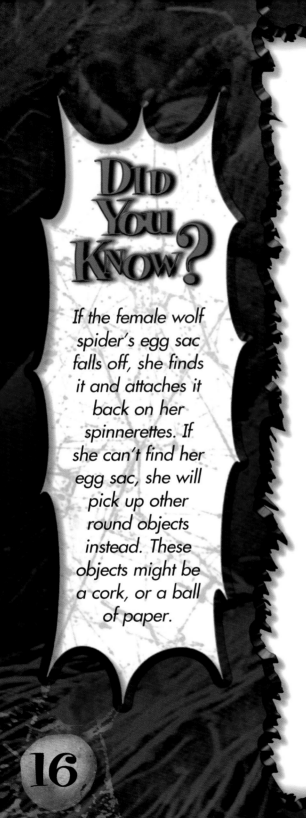

Laying Eggs

Male wolf spiders have interesting ways of attracting mates. Some stand in front of the female wolf spider and wave their legs around. Others rub their bodies across dry leaves or click their legs to make sounds. One wolf spider wraps a fly in silk and gives it to his mate. Each species of wolf spider has a different mating signal so female spiders can recognize their own species.

When she is ready to lay her eggs, the female wolf spider spins a sheet of silk. She lays her eggs on the silk sheet and rolls them into an egg sac. She attaches her egg sac to her spinnerettes and carries it with her.

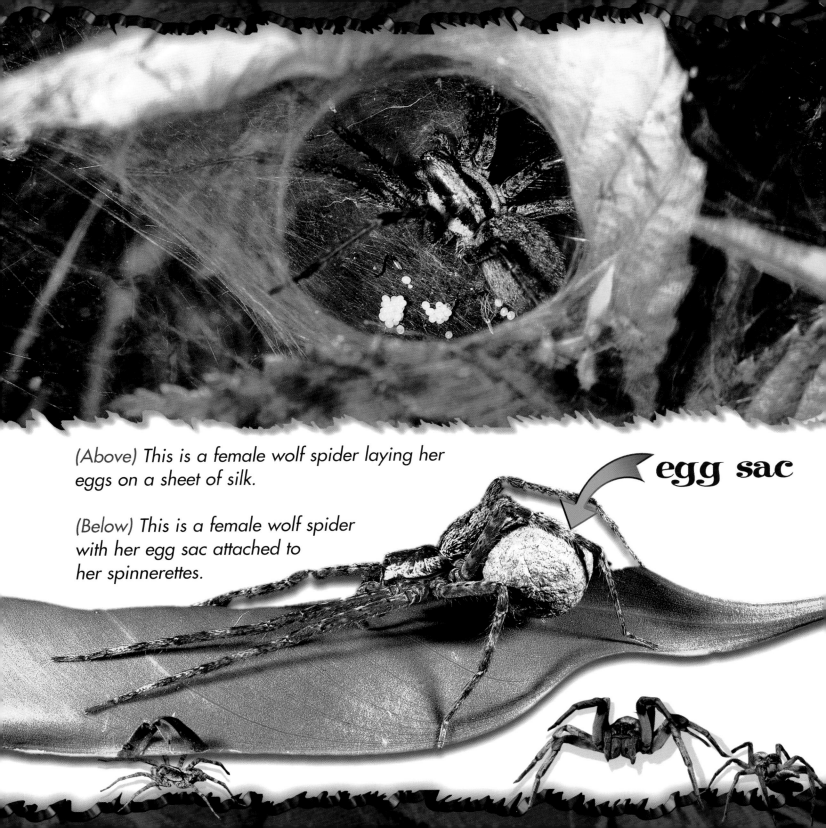

(Above) This is a female wolf spider laying her eggs on a sheet of silk.

(Below) This is a female wolf spider with her egg sac attached to her spinnerettes.

egg sac

(Above) These tiny spiderlings are hatching out of their egg sac, and crawling onto their mother's back.

(Right) This is a mother wolf spider and her spiderlings. The spiderlings are riding around on her back.

Baby Wolf Spiders

A few weeks after the eggs are laid, they hatch. The female spider tears open the egg sac, and many tiny white **spiderlings** climb out. The spiderlings scramble up their mother's legs and onto her back. They hold tight to her hair as she chases prey. The spiderlings do not eat while they are on the mother spider's back. However, they may climb down to get a drink when the mother spider stops for a drink. The spiderlings will ride around on their mother's back for about a week. Then they will race away to begin their own lives.

As the spiderlings grow, their hard exoskeletons become too tight. Their old skin splits and they climb out. This is called molting. The spiderlings will molt many times before they are fully grown.

The Wolf Spider's Enemies

DID YOU KNOW?

Wolf spiders also camouflage their burrows. Some build trap doors over the entrance. Others build little forts of moss, dirt, silk, and twigs around the entrance.

Wolf spiders have two main enemies. The first one is the mantisfly, who preys on wolf spider eggs. The second one is the hunting wasp. Hunting wasps search for wolf spider burrows, and then sting the spider in its burrow. The wasp then lays an egg on the spider and buries the spider and the egg. When the egg hatches, the baby wasps eat the spider.

The wolf spider's brown or gray body helps it hide from its enemies. It **camouflages** itself, or blends into its surroundings, so it can't be seen.

(Left) This is a pompilid wasp stinging a spider. The spider is not dead, but it is paralyzed and helpless against the wasp.

(Below) This Costa Rican wolf spider and her spiderlings are well camouflaged against the pebbly ground.

Wolf Spiders and People

It is not hard to find wolf spiders, especially those that hunt during the day. You might see them running through piles of leaves and around rocks. Wolf spiders may bite if they are picked up. Luckily, wolf spiders in the United States are not known to be poisonous to people.

Wolf spiders are helpful to people because they eat insects. In California, rice farmers bring wolf spiders to their fields to eat insects that are harmful to their crops. Each wolf spider eats between 5 and 15 harmful insects a day. The wolf spiders help the farmers get rid of almost all the insects that destroy their crops.

Glossary

abdomen (AB-doh-men) A spider's rear body part.

Arctic (AHRK-tick) The cold region around the North Pole.

arthropod (AHRTH-roh-pod) A member of the group of animals called Arthropoda.

camouflage (KAHM-uh-flahj) Having the same colors as the environment, in order to blend in and not be seen.

cephalothorax (sef-uh-low-THOR-ax) A spider's front body part made up of its head and chest.

exoskeleton (EX-oh-skel-eh-ton) The hard outer shell of a spider's body.

joints (JOYNTZ) Places where two parts of the body join together.

silk gland (SILK gland) A gland in the spider's body that makes silk.

species (SPEE-sees) Groups of animals or plants that are very much alike.

spiderlings (SPY-der-lings) Baby spiders.

spinnerettes (spin-uhr-ETZ) Organs located on the rear of the spider's abdomen which release silk.

tropics (TRAH-picks) The hottest places on earth near the equator.

vibrate (VY-brayt) To shake.

23

Index

A
abdomen, 8
anthropod, 7
Arctic, 4

B
brain, 8

C
camouflage, 20
cephalothorax, 8

E
eggs, 16
exoskeleton, 7

eyes, 11

H
heart, 8

J
joints, 7

L
lungs, 8
Lycosidae, 7

P
prey, 15

S
silk glands, 8
spiderlings, 19
spinnerettes, 8
stomach, 8

T
tropics, 4

Web Sites

To learn more about wolf spiders, check out these Web sites:

www.ipm.iastate.edu/ipm/iin/swolfspi.html
www.kwic.com/~pagodavista/wolfspid.html

24